I'd like to dedicate this book to my daughter, Adrena, as well as my family and co-workers, Lydia and Lea. Adrena, thank you for being so understanding about all the hours I spent writing instead of playing with you. Lydia and Mom, thank you for taking part in to my vision for the book and business and letting me take the time to write instead of chit chat.

A practical guide for Americans
to save money on insurance, while
protecting their family's financial future

The Great Insurance
SCAM

Martin J. Glennon

Copyright © 2017, Martin Glennon.
All rights reserved.

No part of this book may be reproduced or transmitted in any form or by any means, electronic or mechanical, including photocopying, recording, or by any information retrieval system, without permission in writing from the publisher.

Writing & Publishing Process by PlugAndPlayPublishing.com
Book Cover by Tracey Miller | TraceOfStyle.com
Edited by Jenny Butterfield

ISBN-13: 978-1977837158

ISBN-10: 1977837158

Disclaimer: This book contains opinions, ideas, experiences, and exercises. The purchaser and/or reader of these materials assumes all responsibility for the use of this information. Martin Glennon and Publisher assume no responsibility and/or liability whatsoever for any purchaser and/or reader of these materials.

Table Of Contents

Read This First 1

Section 1 Scams You Should Know About 5

Scam #1: EFT Installment Fee Scam 7

Scam #2: Insurance Companies Adding More 9
Coverage At Renewal Scam

Scam #3: Undisclosed Lack of Coverage Scam 15

Scam #4: "The Illegal Roof Claim" Scam 19

Scam #5: "Agency Fee" Scam 23

Scam #6: Renewal Fee Scam 27

Scam #7: Bad Parts Scam 29

Scam #8: Low Claim Payout Scam 33

Scam #9: Insane High Coverage Scam 37

Scam #10: Towing Coverage Scam 43

Scam #11: Pay in Full Scam 47

Scam #12: Collections Scam 51

Scam #13: Cheapest Price Scam 53

Section 2 Savings You Should Know About 57

Savings You Can Take Advantage Of Immediately 59

Savings #1: Pay In Full 61

Savings #2: Pay Early 63

Savings #3: Loyalty Can Cost You 65

Savings #4: Unused Vehicles 67

Savings #5: Improper Coverage 71

Savings #6: Raising Your Deductible 73

Savings #7: Good Student Discount 75

Savings #8: What Discounts Am I Not Using? 77

Savings #9: Are you Married? 79

Savings #10: Combine Policies 81

Savings #11: Young Drivers 83

Savings #12: Defensive Driving Course 85

Savings You Can Take Advantage Of Over Time 87

Savings #13: Improve Credit Score 89

Savings #14: Early Quote, Early Pay 91

Savings #15: Save On Life Insurance 93

Savings #16: Lose Weight 95

Savings #17: Keeping an Insurance Company 97

Section 3 Extra Things You Should Know About 99

How To Qualify Your Agent 101

Common Insurance Questions You Want Answers To ... 107

Your Next Steps 121

About the Author 123

Read This First

This book is not some theoretical mumbo-jumbo about how the insurance companies are scamming the American public. Nor is it a book about conspiracies or scams in the general sense.

Instead, this book is a public service announcement and a practical guide to help keep you and your family safe and to help you keep as much money as possible in your pocket while getting the best coverage you need.

You may not agree with me on this, but insurance is important. Important for you and your family. Important for your financial future. And important for your friends, neighbors, and fellow America citizens. Without insurance companies, our nation's financial markets would collapse and there would be total chaos. So, while insurance is not a "fun" topic, it is a necessary topic.

As a whole, the system is not perfect by any stretch of the imagination. There are problems, challenges, and issues with insurance companies and insurance agents. There are holes and flaws within the system.

With that said, this book is not meant to "fix" all the issues with insurance. Instead, this book is meant to bring some of the many flaws to the surface, so you can make the best decisions possible for you and your family.

Will this book change the insurance industry overnight? It's doubtful. But maybe, just maybe, it can raise some red flags that will eventually be looked into and updated to better serve the American public. Only time will tell. In the meantime, and more importantly for you, this book can change your life overnight!

Have you ever heard the phrase, "An educated buyer is a smart buyer"? Buying insurance was never taught to you in school, and if you're like most Americans, your parents never taught this to you either. So, it's not your fault. It's not your fault you don't know what to look for. It's not your fault you don't know the right questions to ask. It's not your fault you don't know the games and "scams" insurance agents and companies are playing on you right now.

It's not your fault. But... buying insurance is your responsibility!

You make the decision where to get your insurance. You decide what coverages fit your budget and your family's needs. Yes, you can and should have a trusted agent help you with this, but ultimately you and you alone are responsible for the insurance you invest in.

And make no mistake, insurance is an investment. The right insurance can relieve unwanted stress and literally save your family's financial future. The wrong insurance can wipe out your savings and ruin your family's future forever.

So, since you're ultimately responsible for your insurance and your family's security, I'm sure you can see why it's important for you to become an educated buyer. That's what this book will do for you. Reading this will help you become an educated buyer of insurance.

When you're done reading this book, you'll know what questions to ask your insurance company and your agent to know if you're getting the best deal, to know if they're playing games with you and 'scamming' you, and to know whether you should trust him or not. In addition, you'll know the answers to commonly asked insurance questions, as well as how to immediately save money on your insurance policy!

So, are you ready to get started and become an educated buyer? Are you ready to save money on your insurance policy, while getting the best coverage possible? Are you ready to set up a wall of protection around your family and your finances?

Let's go!

~Martin J. Glennon

P.S. I know insurance is not a fun subject to talk about (or read about). But I assure you that I've written this book to be a light, easy-to-read book. I've eliminated most of the technical jargon, and I've given you a concise picture of what you need to know to best help you along this journey. Enjoy!

Martin J. Glennon

Section 1
Scams You Should Know About

Martin J. Glennon

Scam #1
EFT Installment Fee Scam

The EFT Installment Fee is when you are having your payment directly drafted from your account every month and there is still an installment fee on your payments. Sometimes the amount is small and sometimes there is no discount for automatic withdraw. Read on to find out what your options are.

How This Scam Works:

With most insurance companies, there is a discount for having payments come out of your checking account automatically. If you do not use this discount, typically you would be paying what's called an installment fee. If you call your insurance company to find out what this installment charge is for, usually you will be told it is for "paper and postage."

Most insurance companies charge $10 every month for this installment charge. This explanation is a little ridiculous because it does not cost $10 to send mail, but that is beside the point. The scam I am really drawing your attention to is when a customer is switched to EFT and they no longer receive bills from the insurance company.

Some of the insurance companies charge a full or partial installment fee even after you have switched to EFT. Well, that does not make sense does it? How can you charge a fee for doing nothing? If the insurance company needs the money, they should raise their rates instead of charging a customer for no reason.

How To Avoid This Scam:

Now that you know, you should be able to gather what to do. If you already use EFT, go check if your insurance company is charging you a full installment charge of $10 or more (if they are, I recommend you switch insurance companies because they probably are charging you for other things too). If you don't have EFT, but want to sign up for that discount, ask a local, independent agent to choose a company with a lower EFT installment charge.

Scam #2
Insurance Companies Adding More Coverage At Renewal Scam

Ever wonder why your rates keep going up when they should be going down? Well, this could be one of the reasons. Every time you renew, you should pay close attention to your coverages. If they are different than on your last policy, then there could be something fishy going on. If suddenly your coverages are higher, this is a red flag.

How This Scam Works:

Over the last five years, I have had hundreds of customers come to me from other insurance companies saying, "The insurance company raised my coverages without asking me." Some insurance agents do this without telling the customer in order to get a bigger commission from that person. Ten dollars extra commission on 3,000 customers per year is a hefty bonus.

However, there are insurance agents who are unaware that an insurance company they represent is scamming customers. I remember when I first started writing insurance policies, one policy I wrote went up twice in a two-year period. I had not considered that this could happen and apologized whole heartedly.

Now five years later, I know there are A LOT of Home Insurance Companies that do this. When asked why, they will usually give you some silly reason, like "We estimated your home value had gone up" or "We raised your Liability by $50,000 because it's company policy to do so."

What you should do next is to look over your current insurance policies and compare the coverages to last year. If the rate went up but there are no other differences, there are a handful of different reasons for this and they are not always scam related. I will explain some of these reasons below using Auto and Home Insurance as examples.

Reason for Rate Increase

Rate Increase for Auto:

1. Crime in your Area:

If more vehicles have been stolen in your area as of late, the rate will go up. Also, if there are a lot of hit and runs this will raise the rate too. Your rate is determined largely by those who are breaking the law. If there are a lot of people breaking the law in your area, the insurance company has to pay out more money and your rate goes up.

2. Uninsured Drivers:

You may feel like blaming your insurance company for raising rates all the time, but you shouldn't. More likely, you should be blaming your dead-beat friend who refuses to keep his insurance active. The largest portion of how a rate is determined is when an insurance company has to pay out for a claim that was not even your fault!

If you get hit by an uninsured driver and you have "uninsured motorist" on your policy, your insurance company will pay to fix your car and sue that person. The problem is that an uninsured person can claim bankruptcy and never have to pay. So, now your insurance company has to take over $20,000 losses daily for legal fees, auto damages, and mostly medical bills. When you consider how many people are breaking the law by driving without insurance and involved in accidents, those bills add up fast. The only way the insurance company recoup those losses is to keep the rate up.

If the losses go from $20,000 daily to $30,000 daily, you can expect a 30% increase to your insurance policy. Who is paying for the uninsured motorist problem? The answer is you, me, and all of us who care to keep our policies active. If a company does not raise its rates accordingly, they will go bankrupt in a very short time.

3. You received a traffic citation or were involved in an accident:

Did you get into an accident or receive a ticket during your last policy period? Your rate will go up with almost every company on the market. Companies that do not raise your rates for those things often charge higher rates or fees somewhere else on your policy to make up for the higher risk of insuring you as a driver.

4. Credit

Did your credit take a hit during your last policy period? If you went into bankruptcy or lost a car that you stopped paying on, your credit will take a huge hit. Not all companies determine a rate based on credit, but typically the most reputable companies will. Good credit = good rates. Bad credit = bad rates.

5. More accidents in your area recently:

A sudden increase in accidents in your zip code will almost certainly raise the rates. This shouldn't come as a surprise to most of you. Many times, if there is a tornado or other event with catastrophic loss to many full-coverage vehicles, a company will raise their rates to recoup their losses.

Rate Increase for Home:

1. Crime in your Area:

Crime partly affects your rate for Home Insurance. If your home is in an area where theft is common and your neighbor's homes are vacant, these areas are usually breeding grounds for problems and your insurance rate will reflect the added risk to the company.

2. Weather Claims in your area:

If there are a lot of claims in your area due to hail or storm damage, this can raise your rate and there is not much you can do about it. The rate is determined on the risk versus reward factor.

The insurance company executives say to themselves, "How can we get as many houses covered as possible with as little claims as possible?" That is where good weather areas will come in to play. Your rates will be lower in areas less prone to lake effect weather, tornados, and flooding. In these areas, insurance companies see a larger profit margin.

How To Avoid This Scam:

To avoid this scam, you will have to keep a vigilant eye on your policies. I recommend you ALWAYS have your declaration page sent to you from the insurance company you are covered by. This piece of paper shows your exact coverages on a specific date of an active policy.

Every time the policy is renewed (every six to twelve months depending on the company), you should get out your old declaration page and compare it to the one you were just given. Compare your declaration page every time you renew and be sure to look at the dates to make sure they are correct. If the rate went up a little bit but your coverages didn't change, the difference is probably for one of the reasons I explained above.

Martin J. Glennon

Scam #3
Undisclosed Lack of Coverage Scam

The way some insurance companies go about covering parts of your property but not all of your property is a huge problem in the industry. Not showing what is NOT covered is a problem.

As an agent, I will call a company and ask an underwriter, "Is this covered?" Then the underwriter will say, "I can't answer that, only an insurance adjuster can."

I will then get transferred and talk to the adjuster, and he'll say, "Do you want to file a claim for this particular thing?" I will say, "No, this is a hypothetical question regarding this property." Then he will tell me, "I am sorry, but we cannot answer that question unless a claim is filed because it is always a case by case basis."

These questions are usually as simple as "Will the sewage pipes under my lawn be covered if they bust in winter time?" or "Does sewer backup coverage cover me if it rains too hard, and the sewer doesn't backed up BUT my yard gets a large pool of water and the water seeps into my basement ruining my furniture?"

See what we deal with? We almost never get a straight answer because companies want to be able to deny coverage on little technicalities.

How This Scam Works:

I will use Home Insurance as the example for this one. Now, here is one of the stories of how I learned about this problem. Prepare to be frustrated.

Back when I started in insurance, I made several mistakes, many of them I paid for literally out of my own pocket. The mistake I am referring to in this case, we will call "The Garage Incident." Years ago, a man came to me for insurance on a couple properties, cars, and motorcycles. He was shopping around for insurance and decided to go with me because he liked me the most.

I was grateful for the opportunity to help him and wanted to impress him. Back then, I thought the most important thing was price, but I would learn the hard way that this should not be the top priority. I chose the least expensive insurance company for him, and he was pleasantly surprised about the price.

All was well and good with these policies for about a year-and-a-half. One night, there was a vicious storm with high winds and hail coming down sideways. This poor gentleman's homes were viciously bombarded and damaged. Both homes were in the same general area and insured with the same company.

This man's rental property had a detached garage, and the roof had blown off. The claims adjuster came, looked at both houses, and told my client that there would be no coverage for the roof of his garage. After spending hours on the phone with adjusters and management, I discovered there was no coverage for any detached garages on rental properties.

I went back and double checked his policy documents. There was no clear wording regarding this coverage or non-coverage in his documents. This was a defining moment. As an experiment, I tried to rerun the home in the same company's quote process, and there was nothing regarding this matter during the quote process either. Yes indeed, other structures were listed as covered on the policy so the garage itself is covered. Just not all of the garage.

As hard as I tried to keep this client, it was too much of a letdown for him, and I could not blame him for leaving. He was one of my favorite customers, and we had become friends through doing business together. Sadly, the lack of clarity from this company caused a rift in our friendship, and to this day, we have not recovered.

Needless to say, I do not write for this company anymore, and I do not know what other things they could have been hiding up their sleeve.

Now that you know about "The Garage Incident," you can go and apply what you've learned to your insurance. Remember, the lowest price does not always mean the lowest coverage, and though it would be hard to know about these kinds of scams without me looking at your policy and telling you, they are possible to discover for yourself. If you own your home, make sure to ask your agent if your roof is covered.

How To Avoid This Scam:

The very first thing you want to have is a great insurance agent. I'm not talking about an agent who remembers your name or lets you pay a day late. I'm talking about an agent who genuinely explains what coverages are and expresses a concern about driving without uninsured motorist, etc. You want an agent who helps the community and uses the business to reach out to people who need help. Those agents are out there and you should look for them because you don't know what you're missing.

Scam #4
"The Illegal Roof Claim" Scam

Every couple years, I run into this topic, and I think you should know what this means for you. There are agents who will do anything to make extra money and do not mind throwing their insurance companies under the bus. Agents operating with integrity will lose some potential customers, but in the end, integrity will bring in more business from customer loyalty. More importantly, it's just plain wrong to make false claims and trick customers.

Let's say you just bought a house, and the roof is 25-28 years old. That old roof really needs replaced and will cost you $5,000 or more to do so. The "illegal roof claim" is when an insurance agent tells you that if you buy an insurance policy from him, he can have your roof replaced and the insurance company can foot the bill. The bill is usually paid without the insurance company's knowledge, but there are just as likely and equal number of cases when they know.

So you buy the policy, and your agent makes the claim after a couple weeks. You end up paying for the new roof in one way or another. If the insurance company knows what is happening, they are probably just planning to double your insurance rate after the claim. If they don't know what is happening, you run the risk of getting stuck in a bribery scam between a crooked adjuster and someone shady who will come to your house and damage the roof in a way that looks like it was not natural wear and tear.

How This Scam Works:

The first time I ran in to this was about six years ago. I was working at my father's insurance agency, and at the time, I had a friend buying a new house. It was a beautiful home and was mostly up to date. The only problem was that the roof needed to be replaced. The roof hadn't been replaced in about 25 years.

We quoted the house and let the clients know the roof would need to be replaced. Replacing a roof is no small ticket item, but these kinds of expenses come along with buying a new home. After our quote was given, my friend found another insurance agent who swore their company could pay to put on a new roof. The insurance would be more, but at least my friend would get a new roof out of it.

This sort of thing was a red flag to my father, who had all the experience to see the sham for what it was. My friend started the policy anyway, and after a short time, his new agent filed a claim stating hail damage. The roof was replaced and that was that.

Only, that would not be the end of their problems. After the claim, the rates went up and the agent got a higher commission. This kind of dishonesty is a problem in insurance these days, and you really have to be careful about who you do business with.

How To Avoid This Scam:

What you'd want to do in this case is avoid going with an insurance agent that says he can replace your roof for you. That offer might sound nice at the time, but paying double the rate on your Home Insurance for three to five years because of a claim on your record is not ideal. Also, that agent does not deserve any business if he is willing to operate in a way that is unethical.

Martin J. Glennon

Scam #5
"Agency Fee" Scam

Something people ought to be more aware of this scam because it is more prevalent in some areas of the United States than others. An agency fee is when your insurance agency charges you a "starting policy" fee. This is how some insurance agencies will make extra profit from their customers.

How This Scam Works:

You go to an insurance agency and ask for a quote. On top of what is the normal down payment to start that policy, the agent tells you there is an added $10, $25, or sometimes even $50 higher than what is supposed to be paid. Now I am not saying that charging an agency fee is a scam, as much as I would say charging for it unbeknownst to the customer is a scam.

If an insurance agency has an agency fee, and they feel they rightly deserve the extra money for their services, they may go right ahead and charge the fee. However, they need to have some sort of notice up in the office regarding the fee. The notice needs to be BIG, it needs to be legible, it needs to be pointed out at the time of sale, and it needs to be in plain words that anyone can understand.

Note: If you are in insurance right now and charge a fee but don't tell the customers, here is my advice: Tell the customers.

Tell them plainly and explain what it's for. If you feel you're worth the fee, that's okay, just plead your case to the customers and let them decide. It is unethical to charge a fee that is not plainly stated.

How To Avoid This Scam:

What you should do to avoid this is to speak to your insurance agent, if you have one, and ask if there is an "Agency Fee," "Start-up Fee," or any kind of fee regarding your insurance policy that is not charged by the insurance company, but the insurance agency itself. If the agency does not charge any fees, you are all good and you do not need to think about it anymore.

If your agent says "Yes," ask if the extra charge is posted somewhere and if he commonly brings that up during the sale. If the fee is posted somewhere and you did not notice it when you purchased, you can decide if you want to take responsibility for paying that fee or not. If your agent says that the agency does tell their customers about the fee and you don't remember seeing a notice, you could ask someone else you know who gets insurance through that agency.

If your insurance agent says, "No," it is not posted but the agency does charge an agency fee. I believe you should go somewhere else because this discrepancy means the agency knows that their agents are being dishonest, and the agency was trying to get away with the dishonesty. It also means this insurance company is likely charging for other things you don't know about and that is seriously not cool.

The Great Insurance Scam

I met an agent once that told me her insurance agency charges $10-20 for every new insurance policy. Also, if the customer's policy is cancelled for non-payment, the agency would charge the client another $10-15 to get the policy reactivated on top of what the payment was, or the agency would force the client to start a new policy and charge $10-20 for that.

The worst part about this scam was the agency did not post anything about the fees in the office and there was no consistent price. The agency charged whatever they wanted, whenever they wanted, and split the fee with the owner. When I told a specific agency what I thought about this fee, I was told that in the state of Illinois, almost all insurance agencies charge an agency fee of at least $25. I cannot personally confirm this claim because I have not bought a policy from an agent in Illinois, but the point is to be aware and ask questions.

A key indication that this scam might be happening to you is if your insurance agent will only accept cash or if the agent has his own card swiping machine. A card swiping machine is convenient, but the machine has a processing fee.

Note: If the agent is using a card swiping machine, this can also mean the insurance company sponsoring the agency will not accept cards. You do not want to be with an insurance company who does not accept credit cards because the company is too cheap to have cards accepted on their website.

Martin J. Glennon

Scam #6
Renewal Fee Scam

I mentioned this briefly earlier in the Agency Fee Scam section. The Renewal Fee Scam is when an insurance company or insurance agent charges you a fee at renewal just for keeping your policy with them. This fee is ridiculous and likely indicates financial problems with the company.

How This Scam Works:

You've had your insurance company for six months to a year, and now it is time to start a new term. When you renew, you are confirming you'd like to continue for another six months or a year. Your renewal payment is usually higher than your other payments. Only, there can be different reasons for this higher price.

You'll want to take a look at your insurance declaration page to see if you're being charged this fee. There are two ways that you can be overcharged at renewal. First, confirm there is a rate increase from last term, which would usually be $10-25 increase. This increase is usually a renewal fee, and that fee should be somewhere on the declaration page stating the company is charging a renewal fee.

The second case where you might come across this problem is with your insurance agent. The insurance agency might charge an agency fee. Many insurance agencies who charge a fee for buying policies with them also charge fees for renewing the policy or continuing to stay with them. I think this is a problem because if the agency needs more money, then the agents are doing something wrong.

Customers will come to you as an agent if you operate with integrity.

How To Avoid This Scam:

To avoid this scam you will have to flat out ask your agent what fees are charged. You may need to ask about specific fees. Try asking the questions I've given you below.

"Is there an agency fee if I buy insurance from you?"

"Do you or the insurance companies you represent charge a fee for renewal?"

Most insurance companies charge a fee of some kind, but that is for every policy, not just the renewal. The real problem we're looking for is the renewal fee or agency renewal fee. If they do charge a fee, you'll have to decide for yourself if you want to go somewhere else.

Scam #7
Bad Parts Scam

Now I should note, while this scam is pretty common, you should be more suspicious of your mechanic than your insurance agent. If a mechanic promises a low price (much lower than other shops) and the adjuster recommends you go with this mechanic, then you can be looking at problems regarding your vehicle's replacement parts. You drive away from that mechanic with a fixed car, but the car breaks down a few months later or the aftermarket parts do not work well.

How This Scam Works:

Here is a story I made up in order to give you better understanding of how the scam works.

David has insurance with XYZ Company. One day, David is in an accident and contacts his insurance agent to find out what to do. The agent tells him two things need to happen next: first, David needs to find out what it will cost to repair his vehicle, and second, David will need to find out who is showing "At Fault" on the police report for the accident.

Why these things? Well, if the cost of repair for your vehicle is low, putting in a claim for the damage is not worth the trouble because the claim can raise your insurance cost in the future. Also, if the other driver is showing "At Fault" for the accident on the police report, you do not want to tell your insurance company about the situation unless the other driver is uninsured. If David is showing "At Fault" he will need to let his insurance company know in order to pay for the other person's vehicle and injuries.

For this story, let's say David was "At Fault" and has full-coverage. David takes his vehicle to the body shop that the insurance company suggested. The mechanic takes pictures, looks over the damage, and gives an estimated price to fix the vehicle. David is not sure about the estimate and decides to get a second opinion from another mechanic. He comes to find out that the recommended shop is a significantly lower in price. The claims adjuster urges David to go with the least expensive option from the shop the insurance company sent him to.

The vehicle is fixed, and David leaves the shop with a car that looks repaired. A few months later, the part placed in the vehicle goes bad. He takes his vehicle back to the shop recommended by his insurance company, but the shop won't replace the bad part for free and the insurance company will not pay to replace the part again because the "claim is already closed." I put that statement in quotes because it is common to hear this from a claims adjuster. That is the Bad Parts Scam.

How To Avoid This Scam:

It is difficult to avoid this scam but not impossible. Taking your vehicle to several body shops is a good idea because many estimates showing that one of the repair rates to be impossibly low will give you a better chance at a higher settlement. The higher settlements usually involve the better parts, but not always.

I've had bad experiences with mechanics in the past, so to avoid this scam, I'd ask for a written statement from the mechanic stating the parts are of good quality, and also ask for a written warranty for the parts put in the vehicle. If a mechanic is unwilling to guarantee his work, then I will not do business with him. I guarantee my work as often as possible because the guarantee shows I believe my work to be worthy of a promise.

Note: Many people make the mistake of thinking something can be fixed easily because they do not have the necessary knowledge of how the vehicle needs to be fixed. Some repairs are not as simple as they seem to be. Also if you are not a mechanic, then you would most likely not understand what the laws are regarding repair garages and the process between them and the state.

Some parts must be replaced because of assumed damage. Much like when you've hit your head wearing a motorcycle helmet, after the incident, the helmet is no longer useful because it is meant for single-use protection and would be too dangerous to be used the next time. In the case of the safety of you and your family, "the cheapest price" is not the best way to handle fixing a vehicle that needs vital parts replaced.

Martin J. Glennon

Scam #8
Low Claim Payout Scam

The Low Claim Payout Scam would be anytime when a company uses small excuses to not pay the full amount on a vehicle or house.

How This Scam Works:

Let me give you a scenario that shines a little light on the insurance claims adjuster and what he or she is hired to do. It will be easier to understand the scam in the shoes of the person who has to file the claim. Adjusters have a lot of pressure on them to keep their payout on claims as low as possible.

For years, I have taken pictures of my clients' full-coverage vehicles. Starting out, I did this to protect my clients against their vehicles being stolen so I could send pictures of the vehicle to the police if the vehicle was stolen. This is still the main reason I photograph my clients' cars, but theft and protection are no longer the full reason.

Now, the more serious reason I take pictures of the customer's vehicle is because I do not trust claims adjusters to always be fair to my clients. I am on the side of the people who trust and respect me. My clients come to me because they want to be protected and dealt with in an honest manner. Many of my clients could find a better rate somewhere else but do not want to because they do not want to lose the opportunity to be properly protected.

In the adjusters' defense, their bosses are demanding they find ways to lower payout in claims. So, the insurance adjuster will say he cannot pay the full amount because of prior damage on the vehicle. When the insurance claim's adjuster says, "There seemed to be prior damage on that part of the vehicle, so we are giving a replacement cost of the damaged part" I can then show them pictures and say "This vehicle had no damage" or "This vehicle had minimal damage."

Many times, I wondered how adjusters could be so fickle about a small piece of damage. Whether the damage was there or not should not matter when you have to replace that piece anyway. You see what us insurance agents deal with some times!? Insurance adjusters do this with homes too, so you also need to be aware if you're a home owner. The scam this simple: you have a pipe burst in your home, and the insurance adjustor says the pipes were not up to code then pays you a lower settlement.

All of this said, I believe the insurance adjustor position to be very difficult, frustrating, and hard to change. To pay out on every claim, the insurance company would have to raise insurance prices. If every customer kept his or her policy paid and did not cancel, the company could lower their prices again, but then we'd be right about where we are now. It is easier to control not paying out on every claim than it is to control every customer keeping an active policy.

How To Avoid This Scam:

Be upfront about the damage to your vehicle from the start. Many times, your agent will know how to have the damage fixed quickly and will have access to many repair specialists or mechanics. If the damage on a car can be fixed relatively quickly at a low cost before any claims have occurred, this is your best option to keep your insurance rate low.

For a home, you should consider paying a professional home inspector to inspect your home. Make sure everything is up to code, and you will have no problems from your insurance company if there is a claim. If there are problems, you have the professional inspection paperwork to back up your argument.

Martin J. Glennon

Scam #9
Insane High Coverage Scam

In regards to this scam, I'm not talking about the guy who wants to make sure he and his family are protected against anything. That is a good thing! My favorite speaker to listen to is Jim Rohn, and he has a quote describing this kind of attitude and this kind of person: "Build a financial wall around your family so big that nothing can get into it." If over-insuring you and your family is your way to protect them, there is nothing wrong with that.

What I mean by being scammed for "Insane High Coverage" is when an insurance agent sees someone who has an obviously low-priced life style (i.e. a vehicle worth $5,000, who is single and lives in an apartment), yet the agent gives that person $1,000,000 coverage for everything. Considering this client's lifestyle, it would not be in his best interest to be insured that high. When I quote a customer, I always keep appropriateness in mind and offer the customer the option to raise coverages if desired.

I don't like insurance agents who swindle customers into spending way more than they have to. Insurance is not meant to be the biggest expense you have (Disclaimer: If you're driving record is bad, that is probably the reason insurance is the highest bill you have). Insurance is supposed to be there to protect you from the inevitable, from accidents, and from things outside your control. Insurance is meant to make you whole after a loss, not to make you rich or change your lifestyle.

How This Scam Works:

Let's have a pretend meeting, where I will show how the scam is done. I'll be insurance agent, Dave, and the other character will be you.

Here's the setting:

Imagine you just moved to town after receiving some money left to you by a parent who passed away. You are needing renter's insurance for your apartment and the belongings inside, approximately $14,000 in value. You also have a $4,000 car and a pet needing injury coverage for at least $100,000, which is also required by your apartment complex. You walk in to my office that you saw down the street from your apartment.

Dave: "Welcome to Dave's Insurance Specialists! How may I help you?"

You: "I just moved to town, and I'm looking for a quote on insurance for my apartment, a pet, and my vehicle"

Dave: "Wonderful, my name's Dave. Come have a seat. What's your name?"

You: "My name is Sam. What companies do you represent?"

The Great Insurance Scam

Dave: "Nice to meet you Sam. I work for ABC Company. They are a stock owned company, which means they are owned by regular everyday people like yourself."

You: "Interesting, well, what do you need from me?"

Dave: "Please hand me your ID, the registration for the vehicle, and tell me a little bit about yourself."

You: "Well, my family member just passed away, and left me some money. I decided I needed a change and moved into town for work."

Dave: "Am I the first insurance agent you have spoken to?"

You: "Yes. I just moved in yesterday."

Dave: "You came to the right place first, good for you."

You: *Nervous laugh*

Sometime much later, after small talk completely unrelated to the insurance...

Dave: "Well, that's it, we're all finished with the quote. The down payment is $XX. Would you like to pay with cash, check, or debit?"

You: *Thinking: *Is that price good? Well, I don't know, he seemed nice enough. I'll just go with it and move on.*

"I'll pay with cash Dave."

Dave: "Great, sign in these spots, here are your documents, and I'll see you next month.

You: "Thank you!" *Thinking: Wow, nice guy. Glad I stopped in. That was easy.*

End Scene

Now, I am going to point out the things missing in this discussion. That discussion seemed okay, didn't it? It was pleasant enough, and many customers would love to have that kind of encounter with their agent.

But here are five things missing from this conversation that make could make this discussion and insurance purchase a problem or you in the future:

1. Dave did not mention the amount for the coverages on the policies at all.

2. Dave did not find out what you needed, he wrote what you wanted. In my opinion, this shows a lack of empathy for you, his customer.

3. You have no idea what you're paying for. Does the policy have uninsured or full-coverage and does the renters' insurance include electronics?

4. Dave did not ask if there were other drivers who live with you. This oversight is a huge risk to your future well-being and could mean a claim will not be paid.

5. Dave did not tell you what you're signing. This is a legal binding document and could be used AGAINST you in a court of law. Read what you're signing, and if you don't understand the document, ask questions.

Now let's complete the story by finding out what Dave sold you. Two years later, you have a $3,000 claim for your apartment because some stuff was stolen. Dave tells you that the policy doesn't have theft coverage and nothing would be paid for. You accuse him of scamming you, and he says you never asked him so he thought you knew.

You hear from a co-worker about an agency that will go over coverages with you even if you don't buy a policy from that agency.

Then you come to my office to ask about the coverages on your policy. We show you that you are covered for $1,000,000 on Auto and Liability for your pet, and you have a $100,000 renter's policy for your apartment that doesn't even include theft. You are dumbfounded and enraged with Dave but grateful for our time spent showing you what you didn't know. You decide to buy your policies from us, which are ¼ the price because you now have appropriate coverage for what is needed.

How To Avoid This Scam:

I would suggest that if you want to avoid this happening to you, you should ask your insurance agent a lot of questions. You should also look at your coverage to reference what your insurance agent is telling you. Lastly, you could ask other people you know, what they are covered for.

Scam #10
Towing Coverage Scam

What I mean by this kind of scam is that you've paid for towing on your policy and the limit is so low that paying for towing on your policy is practically worthless. With Towing Coverage, you probably have a limit to how many miles you may tow your vehicle.

How This Scam Works:

You paid to have Towing Coverage on your insurance policy if your vehicle breaks down or is involved in a car accident and cannot be driven any more. There are a couple of ways this service can be packaged on to an auto insurance policy. The first way allows you to call the insurance company and they send out a tow truck to take your vehicle to the closest body shop or somewhere else close by. This type of "towing" on your policy is just called "Towing Coverage."

The second way this service is often rendered in insurance is when you pay for the tow truck to come pick up your vehicle, and you send your receipt to your insurance company to reimburse you. This type of "towing" is called "Towing Reimbursement Coverage." In both types of coverage, there are major downfalls to look out for.

It is common with the Towing Coverage that even though the insurance company will pay to have a tow truck take your vehicle somewhere, the destination must be within five miles. This is incredibly inconvenient sometimes, and you may have to call a second tow truck to take your car to a more suitable destination. That second tow will be an out of pocket expense to you.

In Towing Reimbursement Coverage, commonly only a certain amount of the tow will be reimbursed. So in the fine print, when asking for this coverage, you will see the company has noted that when using Towing Reimbursement Coverage, the most the insurance company will pay you back is $75.

Considering the rarity of needing a tow for most people, this coverage may have only cost you $20 on your policy, but now your tow that was $175 has cost you $120 (the net cost of your tow plus the $20 from you policy) because they only give you $75 back. Some might argue this is not a large enough savings to merit having on a policy since you are not reimbursed the entire cost.

How To Avoid This Scam:

Try to avoid insurance companies that do not pay for your entire towing needs. "Roadside Assistance" is what you are looking for. You may also buy a roadside assistance policy from the companies themselves. Look up roadside assistance plans on Google, and you will find the most popular companies in the market with affordable plans for either six or twelve month time periods (i.e. AAA, Nation Safe Drivers, or Nationwide). Also, if you have

Verizon for your phone service, you can pay a little extra to them to be covered for roadside assistance.

Note: "Rental Coverage" is similar to Towing because both "Rental Coverage" and "Rental Reimbursement" are offered by insurance companies and have the same pitfalls I listed above. The way those coverages work is pretty much the same as the towing coverages, but there is not a great way of avoiding the problems in rental coverages. I would suggest preparing for whichever "pitfall" suits you best. You might be able to find rental plans similar to roadside assistance plans, but I have never encountered a plan that would work any better than an auto insurance plan.

Martin J. Glennon

Scam #11
Pay in Full Scam

The "Pay in Full Scam" is when an insurance agent tells you to pay in full but doesn't give you the paid-in-full discount price.

How This Scam Works:

The insurance agent offers you "a better deal" if you pay in full. This offer sounds great and you have the money, so why not? Everyone knows the paid-in-full price is the best price, right? There are times when unethical insurance agents will use this argument to their advantage and trick you into giving them a sweet bonus.

The agent will take the difference between the all-the-payments-added-up price (including monthly installment fees) and the discounted paid-in-full price and keep the money in-between. I made an example below that may help.

12-monthly-payment price with installment fees: $840

12-month paid-in-full price: $660

Amount savings: $180

The agent then tells you that you have to pay $840 to pay in full and the amount he takes (steals) is $180.

People want to think this doesn't happen. Unfortunately, I know that it does happen. I've seen this scam before and heard about it many times from customers who called out their insurance agents about the discrepancy.

This scam is often difficult to discover because you have to call the company (not the agency) to find out if your agent scammed you, and the company might not tell you the truth because they want the additional money too. Fortunately for you, I am here to help and tell the truth. Below, I will give you a step-by-step process to find out how to discover the truth without too much hassle.

How To Avoid This Scam:

Here is how you steer clear of this scam.

1. Look at the installment fees and add them up.

2. Look at the price at the bottom of your Declaration Page.

3. Subtract the amount from part 1 from the amount in part 2.

4. If the amount is still positive, that is good. If it's negative, that is bad.

5. If the amount is negative, call the insurance company directly, not the agent, and ask what the cost would be to pay in full. If you already paid in installments, ask what the cost would be if you switched to paying in full.

The Great Insurance Scam

6. If the amount given to you by the insurance company is different by more than $10 in comparison to the amount given to you by your insurance agent, there is a problem.

# Martin J. Glennon

Scam #12
Collections Scam

You can fall prey to this scam if your insurance agent suggests you switch insurance companies before the term of your policy has ended, knowing your current bill will get sent to collections. This scam can hurt your credit if not paid on time and is not the correct way to handle the legal contract your insurance company has with you.

Sometimes, I definitely recommend switching insurance companies if they have majorly wronged you or if their rates are way too high because of a new change on the policy and other reputable insurance companies will charge much less. The way to cancel a policy mid-term is to sign a cancellation. Some insurance companies will charge you for the days you were covered after your last bill, which is understandable.

How This Scam Works:

The agent tells you to switch insurance companies to find a better price. Many times, the agents who do this also charge an agency fee. They will collect an agency fee every time, which means instead of keeping you with the same insurance company and not collecting an agency fee at renewal, they just keep switching your company to collect a bigger fee.

Some insurance companies offer agents an incentive for writing a lot of policies with them, and this practice could lead agents to cancel polices just to reach a goal with an insurance company for a bonus. When telling you to switch, agents know that your previous insurance company is going to charge you a collections bill for the days you were covered by the previous company, but they do not mention the extra bill until you bring it up when it comes to you in the mail. Then when you receive this additional bill, you have to decide to pay the previous insurance company what they're owed on top of your payment to your new company, or to default on the collections bill and let your credit take a hit.

How To Avoid This Scam:

Try not to switch policies mid-term unless you absolutely have to. If you have to switch companies, pay the remaining bill to the company you are leaving, and then sign a cancellation with your previous company. Chances are, your previous company will send you some money back after taking the amount for which they would have sent you a collections bill. Also, you won't be charged an additional late fee for not paying on the policy anymore.

Scam #13
Cheapest Price Scam

The "Cheapest price scam" is when you ask for the cheapest price, but the agent knows the service of the insurance company he is pairing you with will be awful. The "cheapest price" often means the worst service. The worst service sometimes means unpaid claims, meaning claims go unpaid up to six months after claim was started. Bad service can also mean no one is available when you call the office.

A couple key factors in determining a company's trustworthiness are: One, are they available when I call to talk to someone and how long does it take for them to call me back (if ever); Two, how is their pricing in relation to every other insurance company around? If the pricing is the lowest around, that is very dangerous, and you need to drop them as soon as you can.

There are cases where this will not apply. Being qualified for a lot of discounts can get you the lowest price around, and that is not what I mean when I say "lowest price." What I meant is that without applying any discounts to the quote, they offer extraordinarily low pricing in comparison the other companies.

How This Scam Works:

You go to a new insurance office and ask for the cheapest price. You and the agent do not discuss coverages or what that means to have the cheapest price. You buy the policy recommended which does indeed seem to be the lowest price around. An accident occurs, you cannot get ahold of anyone at the claims office, and you have to leave a message.

You ask your insurance agent to get involved because you have not heard from your insurance company in the two days since you left your voicemail. The agent cannot get ahold of the insurance claims office either and has to call someone else in the company. The person tells the agent that someone from claims will be calling you, the customer. You do not hear from the claims office for two days.

The claims adjuster asks what happened in the accident, and you give him the whole story. He says he will call you back after he has determined fault or is able to send someone out to look at your car. You do not hear back from him and have to keep calling them. The insurance adjuster's answering machine says he is out of town, or his machine might also say that a response might take up to 48 hours after you leave a voicemail and to not leave more than one message.

You ask your insurance agent to get involved again. Your insurance agent spends an hour every week trying to help you with this problem for another two months. I think you're starting to get where this is going. Some simple fender bender becomes way more stressful than it needs to be. These are the types of insurance companies I do not sell in my office. If I have a company that starts showing these signs, I end my contract with them because I don't want to spend an hour every week doing what the insurance adjuster gets paid to do.

How To Avoid This Scam:

Never buy the cheapest price in insurance unless you have a bunch of discounts on the policy. Find an agent that is honest and willing to find a good company for you.

Martin J. Glennon

Section 2
Savings You Should Know About

Martin J. Glennon

Savings You Can Take Advantage Of Immediately

My intention for this section is to show you savings you can take advantage of immediately. Some will apply to you and your family, while others will not. Take note of the ones that do apply to you, and start saving today!

In this section, you'll find:

Savings #1: Pay In Full

Savings #2: Pay Early

Savings #3: Loyalty Can Cost You

Savings #4: Unused Vehicles

Savings #5: Improper Coverage

Savings #6: Raising Your Deductible

Savings #7: Good Student Discount

Savings #8: What Discounts Am I Not Using?

Savings #9: Are you Married?

Savings #10: Combine Policies

Savings #11: Young Drivers

Savings #12: Defensive Driving Course

Martin J. Glennon

Savings #1
Pay In Full

I want you to look at your policy amount on the Declaration Page. That page should show the price charged for each coverage and then add them all together for you. I am going to show you a sneaky trick that almost no one ever notices. Ask your agent for an installments page or a breakdown of monthly payments for the remainder of your policy. Grab a calculator, and take a seat.

Are you ready?

Now, add all the installments together and compare them to the premium amount on the Declaration Page. By now you should be noticing a large difference in price between the two amounts. With the installments added together being the larger amount. "How can that be?" you might be thinking. Well, this is because there is a little fee on EVERY STINKING PAYMENT that the insurance company doesn't want you to know about.

Many companies call it a "paper and postage charge" or "installment fee." Now, I don't know if you send mail out, but I definitely do. So often in fact that I know it costs me nowhere near $10-12 to send a few pieces of paper in an envelope with a stamp. Insurance companies are not the only culprits of this scam. The sad truth is that for many of you, this is happening on your utility bills, cell phones bills, and many other places too.

The standard across the insurance industry is $10-12 a month for this fee. But, here's a little secret about this fee. There is a way to keep yourself from paying the extra $120-140 a year from paying in installments. If you can afford to, pay the policy in full! By paying in full, you will avoid all the installment fees and usually get an added discount on top.

Paying up front will bring your paid-in-full price actually below the policy premium amount. This discount is usually 10% off. Some of you might be thinking, "I already knew about that, if I could afford to pay in full I would have." If you were thinking this, I have another little tip for you in the next section.

You should be able to pay your premium off whether you are in the middle of a policy term or just starting. If you do not work with an insurance agent and purchased your insurance online, you should be able to request a pay-off amount by calling. Paying the policy off in full when you are just buying it will save you the most money, but you usually can still save some money by paying off the rest of your premium in full during the middle of your policy term.

Savings #2
Pay Early

The monthly fee is possible to avoid even if you're not paying in full. One of the ways of kicking this fee is paying more than one month's premium at a time. If the insurance company does not have to send you a bill, many times they will not charge you the installment fee. Some companies will still charge the fee even though you've paid ahead, and that is extra scam-y.

To keep the savings trend going, I'd suggest paying the next month even though it is not due. Stay a month ahead if you can, and that will save you the installment fee every month. Mark your calendar and forget about waiting for the bill. If you wait for the bill, the fees are back on and you're right back where you started. You will have to do this process again starting at the next renewal, so a twelve-month plan will save you slightly more in the long run. Check with your agent to find out how much money you'll save each month to pay ahead.

The thing about this discount I like most is that you can start right now. Go online and pay next month, then when your next payment (which you've already paid) would normally be due, pay it again. Continue the cycle, and you're unstoppable. Boom, you now only pay what you have to, and not what they want you to.

Martin J. Glennon

Savings #3
Loyalty Can Cost You

You're not going to hear this from a lot of insurance agents. Most insurance agents work for a captive insurance company. What this means is that the agent is not allowed to sell insurance policies for more than one insurance company. I am an independent insurance agent, and this means I am allowed to sell for as many insurance companies as will let me sell for them.

The reason I titled this section "Loyalty Can Cost You" is because I believe it can hurt you to stay with an insurance company for too long. Two or Three years is my suggestion, because insurance companies often have rate changes. Consider this change like a new election period for the next insurance companies.

Some of the insurance companies give higher discounts for switching than others. Some of the insurance companies will give you better rates on one type of policy (i.e. Home) and the same for your second as your previous company on another type of policy (i.e. cycle or auto). You just don't know until you look around.

That said, I believe having a good relationship with your insurance agent is very important. There are many benefits to keeping someone you trust handling your insurance and you feel has taken good care of you and your family. This is why I am an independent insurance agent. If you have an independent insurance agent you can switch insurance companies, but keep the insurance agent.

Independent insurance agents usually get lower commission than captive insurance agents because they are not specifically loyal to any one company. They have the unique advantage of being able to do what is best for the client. In many cases, what's best for the client means switching companies. Not that captive agents don't do the best that they can, but they can only do as much as they are allowed to.

From my perspective, the lower commission is worth the payoff of getting to make my clients happy with me and my agency. I can maintain a relationship, and they get to keep someone they trust as their agent. If you haven't found a good independent agent, you don't know what you're missing!

Savings #4
Unused Vehicles

This can be a savings in two different ways. One is to add the unused vehicle to your policy, and the other way is to remove a garaged vehicle that is raising your premium. Understanding why removing a vehicle from your policy can lower your premium is easy.

But you're probably thinking, "Adding a vehicle would raise the price because I'm covering more vehicles, right?"

Wrong!

Most insurance companies actually do not charge for the second vehicle if you have full-coverage on the first. Some companies will even lower the price because the fact that you're not only driving the full-coverage vehicle all the time is great news to them.

Insurance companies like this arrangement because it means you are driving the full-coverage vehicle less. Statistically, the likelihood that they will have to pay out a big claim has dropped. Insurance companies often reward you for this by charging very little if anything for the secondary vehicle without full coverage.

However, in some cases, adding an unused vehicle will raise the premium. If you have a second driver on the policy, the company assumes that both vehicles are being driven and has an increase in exposure to consider. Also, if your driving record is bad, this could increase the price of adding a second car because the second car implies you drive a lot. The implication is that you need two cars and are very likely to have a claim on both of those cars.

I am not going to pretend to understand all of the complex pricing algorithms they use to determine your exact price, but it is a mix of many factors. I have talked with several key people at some of the insurance companies I sell for, and they have explained to me some of the pricing details. Below, I've listed four of the big factors that go in to the math of automobile insurance rating to help you better understand how they are calculated.

4 Key Factors in Insurance Rating:

1. Address

Where you live has a lot to do with your insurance rate. For example, if you live in a low-crime area your insurance rates will typically be lower than if you lived in a high-crime area. There are zip codes that have such a low population that companies do not have a rating standard for the area. In these scenarios, insurance companies give the area a flat rate, which may be more expensive than surrounding zip codes that are similar.

2. Your Driving Record

This is the most commonly known Rating Factor. Obviously, the worse your driving record is, the more you pay for insurance. A bad record doesn't mean parking tickets or seat-belt tickets. I'm talking about Driving Under the Influence (DUI's), speeding tickets, accidents without insurance, or running red lights. With most insurance companies, they only charge you for tickets within the last three years. For accidents, they go back five years.

3. Vehicles

If you are just getting Liability on the policy, you can expect your insurance to cost the same for any vehicle you have. A second vehicle will increase the rate. The reason Liability Coverage does not change your rate to switch vehicles for liability is because liability is covering you and your driving, not your car.

Liability only covers the other person's car and people in that car if you're at fault. If you have an expensive car for Liability and switch it for an old car for Liability, your rate should not change. If you have Uninsured Motorist, your rate will change because there is potential the company will have to pay to cover your vehicle if you're involved in an accident with an uninsured driver.

4. Drivers

Pretend you have five people living in your home including yourself. Before adding anyone to your policy, your rate is $63 a month. One of the people in your house is too young to drive, another has his own policy somewhere else and does not drive your car, but the other two people do drive your car. The two that drive your car have vastly different circumstances than yourself as far as the insurance company is concerned.

One of them is only 17, and his age makes your rate go up by $80 a month due to his inexperience regardless of the vehicle you drive. The other driver is 28, so the age is not a problem on your rate, but he has had two DUI's and an accident in the last five years. Ouch, your rate is now up another $120 a month.

So, now your rate is $263! If you had full-coverage, it would likely be $500-$600 a month. There is too much risk in your household and you need to find out some other solution. For this situation, I recommend the young driver be on his own policy with Liability and Uninsured Motorist for an inexpensive car.

Excuse me for being blunt about the other guy, but I believe he should not be driving until he figures out how to drive responsibly. Driving is a privilege, not a right, and he has not proven that he respects the laws or the other people on the road. There is no excuse for driving without insurance or driving while intoxicated.

Savings #5
Improper Coverage

Being over covered is possible. If you are covered for half-a-million dollars for Liability and you don't drive much, paying for that much coverage doesn't make sense. Of course, some insurance agents might argue that you should keep high coverages for just-in-case scenarios.

Personally, I don't keep my liability limits that high because I know the statistical probability of me causing an accident large enough to cause that much injury or property damage. The point is this: you are taking a chance either way. I choose to go with the savings option, but you might choose to err on the side of caution and go with the extra-coverage option.

Another thing to watch out for is having unnecessary coverage on your policy. Some policies could have added pet coverage, some accidental death, and some might have accessory coverage. Keep an eye out for what is on your policy that you don't need and that you can trim off.

Note: One thing that is not required everywhere, but I still recommend having on your policy, is Uninsured Motorist. I am a big believer in this coverage because I have seen people use this coverage so many times. Having this coverage has kept people from going bankrupt. It is one of the most underrated features of insurance, and I think this coverage should be required by law.

Savings #6
Raising Your Deductible

Here is an example of a frequent money-saving action my customers have taken during my time as an insurance agent. These customers raise their deductibles to $1,000, instead of the more popular choice of $500, to save themselves about $20 a month. This is a good option for lowering your rate with a couple exceptions.

One exception is that a lot of lienholders who give you car loans will not allow $1,000 deductible. Some even require as low as $250 deductible, which will significantly increase your payments. Some lienholders consider $500 or $1000 deductible a breach of contract for the sale and will repossess your car. So be sure you have an understanding with your vehicle's lienholder before raising your deductible.

Another exception to the action of raising your deductible is that your vehicle may not be worth very much and raising the deductible means less of a payoff for you if you are in an accident that totals your car.

For example, if you get in an accident in your $1400 car and it is totaled, with a $500 deductible you will get $900. If you have a $1,000 deductible, you will only get $400, which makes raising your deductible really not worth doing in this case.

The final exception I will point out is that $1,000 is considered a lot of money to many people. If your vehicle is worth $5,000 and the damage in an accident is $3,500, the insurance company will pay the repair garage $2,500 and you will have to come up with $1,000 before they will release the vehicle to you. Paying the higher deductible is often easier said than done. Choose your deductible wisely.

Savings #7
Good Student Discount

This is one of the more well-known, saving methods for parents of young drivers. If you have a young driver on your policy and the rate is too high, you can use your child's grades as a discount with most insurance companies.

The typical requirement is a 4.0 or better to qualify. Check with your agent to see if the company you have offers this discount.

Martin J. Glennon

Savings #8
What Discounts Am I Not Using?

Meet with your agent and ask him what you might qualify for to save on your insurance policy. If you own your home, almost all companies give a discount for this because owning shows a more stable person who handles his or her money well.

Some insurance companies offer discounts for cars that are not driven often. You can have your insurance documents sent as an email instead of through the regular mail to save the mailing fee that most of the bigger insurance companies charge.

A great discount I suggest is Automatic Withdraw or EFT (electronic funds transfer) for your payments. EFT will save you time and money because you don't have to drive to the insurance office to make your payment and the insurance company does not need to send you a bill.

These are just some of the discounts available. All of the discounts above will require proof (i.e. proof you did not drive a certain car much, proof of your email, proof you own your home, etc.).

Savings #9
Are you Married?

If you recently married but have a separate policy from your spouse, you are almost always paying more for insurance than you need to be. If you are not listed as married on your policy, you are missing out on some savings.

Insurance companies don't call this savings a "discount" because they require proof for discounts.

Just simply have you and your spouse listed on the policy, and the rate will go down after the status is switched from "single" to "married."

Additionally, if you have separate policies and combine the two cars onto one of the policies, the second car will get a multi-car discount. The only case when this is not a good idea is when one spouse has a poor driving record.

Martin J. Glennon

Savings #10
Combine Policies

Say there are four drivers in your household. Each of them has his own insurance policy. Each of them pays a policy fee with the insurance company to start the policy. Each of them pays an installment fee every month. You own your home and have a discount on your policy, but none of the others do.

With this scenario in mind, I can say almost without a doubt that you could be saving more. If all four drivers were on your policy, the combined policy would have three multi-car discounts, a homeowner's discount, and only one policy fee with one installment fee. If this circumstance applies to you, go try combining policies to see if your savings is significant enough to make the change.

The only exception you may find is with a young driver. If you have a younger driver on your policy, this may not be the best option for you. You will most likely still want to keep the young driver on his own policy. We'll look at that in this next tip…

Martin J. Glennon

Savings #11
Young Drivers

As I have mentioned previously, placing young drivers on their own insurance policy is the best method to keeping your cost lower. What I mean by "young drivers" is any driver in your household below the age of twenty. Putting them on an insurance policy with full-coverage insurance will raise your rate tremendously.

The way I would usually handle a young driver is by writing an insurance policy for them with just Liability and Uninsured Motorist on a cheap car. This way, your rate is unaffected and they get to keep driving. A driver under 20 basically has no driving experience, and the choices they make while driving are dangerous.

Here are a couple interesting statistics that confirm this statement:

- Studies show that young people send or receive a text every six minutes.

- Studies show that accidents caused by young drivers are much more severe because of the reckless driving habits (i.e. driving too fast, fast driving in rain or snow, trying to beat trains).

Martin J. Glennon

Savings #12
Defensive Driving Course

There is a discount with a lot of insurance companies if you just go take a Defensive Driving Course through the Bureau of Motor Vehicles. Simply bring the certificate for taking the course to your agent or send the certificate to your insurance company, and the discount will be applied.

If you have a bad driving record, this would be a good idea for you to try and lower your rate. I've seen the price for this program be as low as $40.

Martin J. Glennon

Savings You Can Take Advantage Of Over Time

My intention for this section is to have you think long-term savings. These are some strategies that I like to call "The Long Cons" in which you will set yourself up for savings in the future with things you implement in the present.

In this section, you'll find:

Savings #13: Improve Credit Score

Savings #14: Early Quote, Early Pay

Savings #15: Save On Life Insurance

Savings #16: Lose Weight

Savings #17: Keeping an Insurance Company

Martin J. Glennon

Savings #13
Improve Credit Score

Simply put, you can improve your insurance rate by improving your credit. This strategy works for both auto and home coverages. The companies that offer the most savings with great coverage require great credit.

Improving your credit is easy enough. Have no more than two credit cards, use them at least once a month, never miss a payment, and pay them off when you pay your bills (or as soon as you can).

Buying a car is another way to improve your credit. The rules are similar as in don't miss payments, pay on time, and pay it off. I think you get the point. If your credit is bad now, you can fix your credit score within five years and your insurance rate will go down once your score is fixed.

Martin J. Glennon

Savings #14
Early Quote, Early Pay

Do you have a renewal coming up? Here's what you should do. Go to your insurance agent, ask for him to requote your insurance policy 20 days ahead of time and tell them to only pick a company that offers advanced quote discount.

When they get back to you, make sure you pay for the new insurance policy at least 10 days before the renewal date, and you have just saved yourself a bunch of money for minimum effort.

If you are with a captive insurance agent, I am sorry but this saving strategy will not apply to you unless you are leaving your agent's company. Since I am an independent insurance agent, I can do this with my clients in order to leverage their savings. I also want to point out that, as far as I know, this discount only applies to auto insurance policies.

Savings #15
Save On Life Insurance

This saving strategy is specific to Life Insurance and smokers. Not a huge majority of people are affected by this tip, but maybe you can pass the word on to those who'd find it useful.

For a smoker, Life Insurance is way more expensive. The statistics show a sad future for those who smoke, and so the insurance companies are justified in their price increase to cover them.

However, this doesn't mean you can't save long term. A person who quits smoking for just one year will be able to cut their price in half with most Life Insurance companies.

That's a big deal! You have a family who depends on your income and health. The price cut helps a lot.

Martin J. Glennon

Savings #16
Lose Weight

Okay, so I showed you how to save on life insurance by quitting a bad habit, but how about improving yourself in a physical way? If you are able to start exercising more and lose weight this will improve your Life Insurance as well, not to mention many other facets of your life will improve as well.

The price will not drop as much as someone who quit smoking, but losing weight will still lower your rate.

Martin J. Glennon

Savings #17
Keeping an Insurance Company

This is sort of a counter-intuitive method to one I've described earlier, so let me explain. The method I explained earlier in the book talks about switching companies every few years if your current company is raising your rates.

It's your money and you want to save where you can while still getting the same coverage, so I'm sure this advice makes sense to you.

However, some insurance companies incrementally lower your rate at every renewal for being a loyal customer. The reason is simple: these companies know that a loyal customer is worth more to them over time, so they reward you for sticking with them.

Therefore, the most loyal and reliable customers get the best rates and the best service. So to get the best rate and service with these insurance companies, be loyal and reliable and you will be rewarded.

Martin J. Glennon

Section 3
Extra Things You Should Know About

Martin J. Glennon

How To Qualify Your Agent

I wanted to write a preface to this section for you in order to express the importance of what I am about to delve into. In this section, I am going to tell you what I consider to be a great insurance agent. I will tell you how to approach getting a new agent, what getting a new agent means for you if you do, and how to choose the best agent out there.

By now, most of us have heard about the horrors of the insurance industry, and I agree there is a problem. There is corruption, greed, and a general lack of disregard for what is important to each individual. In a way, the respect and finesse of a good agent is dying, and that fact saddens me. It saddens me because the major draw for me to become an agent myself was that I could get paid to help people. I could listen to their life challenges and help when I am able.

There was a time when insurance agents funded most little league and soccer teams in the area, a time when being an agent meant you were a community friend who looked out for people and made sure the community's needs were fairly dealt with and met. There was a time when you knew if something was happening to you and your family, you could count on your agent to help you out.

One of my favorite speakers is Jim Rohn. In one of his speeches, he discussed the importance of a good insurance agent. Jim called his agent once in the dead of winter after his furnace went out. The agent brought him firewood for the fireplace and helped him handle the claim. Jim said he was so impressed with the agent that he promised himself he would never switch again, and the agent was still a family friend twenty years later.

Most insurance agents now are just in business for the money. I think that's a shame and believe agents need to return to adding value to their customer's lives. Below is a list of qualities you want to look for in order to find an agent who has the qualities that will add the most value to you and your family.

10 Rules To Qualifying Your Agent:

1. Do not just pick the first agent you talk to.

This is not a blanket statement. When you are searching for a new insurance agent, you should call at least five different places to get a quote. If the first agent you talk to has the most redeeming qualities, then you should go with him.

2. Choose an insurance agent who explains coverages to you without you asking.

This is something the majority of insurance agents do and customers don't realize it. Earlier in the book, I went over a bad conversation you might have with an agent if you just moved in to town and walked into an agency. That conversation illustrates exactly the point that I'm trying make here. You want an agent who is going to explain coverages to you or, at the very least, ask you if you understand your coverages before selling you an insurance policy.

3. Do not pick an insurance agent who charges an upfront fee.

A lot of agents will say "Well, I am worth it" or "It deters the bad customers from buying from me," but I disagree. We all know the added fee is a ploy to make more money and it's unnecessary. Insurance companies pay their agents, and if we improve our performance, we can negotiate a higher commission. There are plenty of great agents/agencies who will charge you no fee and still offer fantastic service.

4. Choose an insurance agent who tries to get to know you personally.

This is really important. You have to really like this person who is about to become your agent. If you feel like an agent is scamming you, go somewhere else. You don't have to stay with someone who does not take an interest in you and your personal life. I like to go visit my customers in the hospital, call them on their birthdays, or congratulate them if there is a birth in their family.

5. Do not choose an insurance agent based on the price alone.

Hands down, this is the biggest mistake customers make when buying a new policy from an agent they don't know. The best price is not the answer to your money woes. The best price is not the best service or quality. You want a claim done in one week? That is not a cheapest price company. You pay for quality and good service, and it's a fair trade.

6. Do not choose an insurance agent who does not call you back or does not respect your time.

Something I hear far too often from clients is "I chose you, because you called me back." Why in the world would you keep an agent who has no respect for your time? We have a rule in my office that if someone leaves a message before we close the office for the day, we call them back before we leave, always.

7. Keep an insurance agent who does not break promises.

Obviously in this case, you will need to work with the agent before finding out if he has this quality. Ask for a promise every now and then, like a committed date and time for something to be done. This will give your agent an opportunity to prove himself. If he doesn't keep promises, you can't really count on him when something important comes up like an accident or a claim.

8. Choose an insurance agent who is honest about coverages and benefits.

Ask your agent if the coverages you have are good for you and your family. Look at your policy or quote, and check if there are any things added that your agent did not tell you about. This is a good indication that he will be adding little things to your policy in the future, and you should think about getting a new agent.

9. Keep an insurance agent who is willing to help with the claim.

Every now and then, I have to help a customer with a claim. Sometimes, I will help because the customer has never had a claim before or because the adjuster is not returning phone calls.

This is really one of the main functions of being an insurance agent, and to offload this responsibility to someone else is a bit of laziness. I'm not saying I will file a claim for my clients, but helping someone who has paid me to be covered in an unfair or challenging situation is how I define being a "good agent."

10. Keep an insurance agent that is happy to see and hear from you.

This is simple enough. If the agent seems to care less whether you're insured with him or not, then what's the point? Go somewhere you will be appreciated. Let the agent who deserves your business get your business.

Martin J. Glennon

Common Insurance Questions You Want Answers To

This section is at the heart of all the work I do to help my customers better understand what matters in insurance and why we operate under certain rules that can look suspect to those who don't understand them.

My aim is to spread better understanding about the insurance industry. The questions that follow are, in my opinion, the questions that you should be asking and how I would answer if we were speaking in person.

What coverages do you recommend for an older car?

This can be a difficult question to answer because, in the end, how much coverage to carry is a client's personal choice. First I would say, start with coverages at least at 25/50/25 for Liability, and always have Uninsured/Underinsured motorist with matching limits to Liability. I already explained those coverages briefly in the book elsewhere, but I'll explain them for you again.

First of all, Liability means you are covering the other driver's medical bills, the medical bills of his passengers, and damages to the other vehicle. This coverage is meant to protect you from a lawsuit if you cause an accident. You're Liability coverage on proof of insurance will always read in some variation of three numbers like this 25/50/10.

You might be confused if yours is different. Yours could say 100/300/50 or 25/50/25, but the combination is not important right now. The first two numbers relate to the amount your insurance company will pay for medical bills. The first number is the amount they'll pay for EACH person injured ($25,000), and the second number is the TOTAL amount they'll pay for all the injuries ($50,000).

Let's look at three simple examples using the coverages 25/50/10, assuming that you are at fault in each accident in these examples:

Example #1: You've caused an accident with ONE car and the driver of the car sustains $18,000 in medical injuries. Your company will cover them completely since the company will cover up to $25,000 (**25**/50/10) in medical bills for each person in the accident.

Example #2: The accident you caused involved TWO cars besides your own, and one person from each of the other cars (TWO PEOPLE) was injured. Each of the two other drivers have medical bills reaching $20,000. In this case, your insurance company will cover the injuries completely since you've paid to have $25,000 (**25**/50/10) in medical bills per person AND up to $50,000 (25/**50**/10) for total medical bills in any one accident.

Example #3: If you're in an accident with TWO cars and two people from each car (FOUR PEOPLE) sustain injuries of $12,000 each, then your insurance company will cover the injuries completely since the total for each person is below $25,000 per person AND the total of $48,000 in medical bills is less than $50,000 (**25/50**/10).

The third number in the series (25/50/**10**) relates to the vehicle or property (car, boat, house, tree) of the other driver or property owner. So, let's say you're in an accident that you caused and ONE other car is damaged. If that car's damages are less than $10,000 (25/50/**10**), then your insurance company will pay to have the car repaired or replaced. If the damages are more than $10,000, then your company will pay the first $10,000, and you'll be responsible to pay the rest of the damages to the other vehicle.

Now Uninsured Motorist is so very important, so pay close attention. Imagine you were just in an accident and only had Liability insurance, but the other person was at fault. "No problem" you say, "That person's insurance company will have to pay." That's true, but what happens if the other driver did not have any insurance. You might be thinking "Easy, then that person will have to pay." Sadly, it's not that easy, consider all the extra effort you'll have to put in because of this.

Suddenly you are paying for lawyers, court costs, and possibly taking days off of work unpaid to sue the person who hit you. Then you come to find out that the other driver did not have insurance because he didn't have a job, money, or and ability to pay anything whatsoever.

This dilemma is only magnified if you are injured and cannot work. And what if the other driver goes into bankruptcy? You get nothing in most cases!

This is a worst case scenario but actually a very common scenario. We're in a world where we see drama like this daily on the news. Let me tell you a secret. If you have this magic coverage called "Uninsured Motorist," most of these headaches are wiped away.

Your insurance company will find out that Joe Shmo did not have insurance, and your insurance company sends a check for the damage that interrupted your life. This is where you jump for joy in agreement that this coverage has improved your impression of insurance. (If your name is Joe Shmo, I'm sorry for dragging your name through the mud).

NOTE: You cannot have higher Uninsured Motorist limits than Liability, but the coverage may be adjusted to match. Also, if you put Uninsured Motorist on your policy, the agent is likely to put Underinsured Motorist on as well. This coverage is if your medical bills are more than the other driver has coverage for. In the case where the other driver only has $25,000 medical coverage for you and you're injured for $55,000, your Underinsured Motorist will take over and pay the rest of those medical bills. There is a limit to this coverage, so check with your agent to see how much you have.

Is it better to have a bundle policy for Home and Auto than to separate them?

Okay, here's the truth. A lot of agents try to sell you on bundling for a "better deal." While it's true you usually get a discount for putting both policies with the same company, having home insurance with a different insurance company than your auto can save you so much that losing the bundle discount may be worth it. Bundling is a cheap sales tactic.

On top of that, most auto insurance companies also give a discount for owning a home which can save you as much as bundling anyway. With that said, I suggest checking with an Insurance Broker to make sure this saving-tactic is true or false in your circumstance. I have used this unbundling tactic to save my clients money time and time again.

If I have full-coverage does that mean I can drive anyone's vehicle with full-coverage?

This is a common misconception. The coverage this question suggests is called "Any Auto Coverage." Any Auto Coverage is typically only available to repair garages and dealerships because the employees need to be able to drive multiple cars on the job (i.e. test driving, repairing vehicles, etc.).

This kind of coverage is not for everyone, and it is way more expensive than just purchasing insurance for the vehicle you're going to be driving. If you are going to drive someone else's vehicle, first make sure that person has insurance on his vehicle.

I have seen people lose their licenses for trusting the owner of the vehicle has proper insurance, far too many times. Don't let that be you.

I have six cars, but I am the only driver. Should I insure them all?

This is your choice in the end, but my answer would almost always be "no." If you want to keep your cost low and you are the only driver in the household, then only insure the vehicles you are using. The other unused vehicles should be placed in storage. All you're doing by insuring vehicles you don't drive is throwing the money in my pocket for services you don't need, and I don't want to take advantage of you.

If you do drive all the vehicles, absolutely get insurance on all of them because penalties for driving uninsured can range anywhere from losing your license to getting a ticket to higher insurance premiums in the future to lawsuits and bankruptcy.

The price for driving without insurance is very high. In 2014, one out of every 134 people in the USA was injured in a car accident. Most of us pass that many cars on a ten-minute drive to work, so never drive without insurance!

So, to end this topic on an even more personal, serious note, I will reiterate that I only sell a policy if I feel my services are providing value to the person I am working with. I only do win-win scenarios. I sometimes have customers that tell me they drive all their cars at least once a week, but I always tell them they will be paying way more on insurance than they need to before placing insurance on all the vehicles.

If my vehicle is insured, can anyone drive it?

This question has many twists and turns to it. This is a complicated question to answer because it depends on the exact scenario. The answer may surprise you. Here are three scenarios that most people think this situation means, and you try to guess which one is right.

- If I have insurance on my vehicle, my insurance company will cover anyone in my family to drive it, whether that person is listed as a driver or not.

- If I have insurance on my vehicle, my insurance company will cover anyone in the household to drive the vehicle, whether that person is listed as a driver on the policy or not.

- If I have insurance on my vehicle, my insurance company will cover anyone who does not live with me, even if they are not listed as a driver on my policy, as long as I give permission and that permission is not for regular use. Anyone who lives with me has to be listed as a driver to drive my vehicle.

Which did you think the correct answer is? If you guessed the middle answer you are among the majority. Sadly, that answer is horribly wrong, and if you follow that formula, you will end up having financial liability if that driver gets in an accident because the insurance company will not pay for the damages.

The top answer sounds like it could be right, but that is not correct either. There are too many variables to insuring "anyone in your family" because your brother could have two DUI's while you have a perfect driving record. Do you think he should be allowed to drive your car without paying anything considering his past record? When we ask these questions, we start to understand more why insurance is the way it is, as frustrating as it may be at times.

The correct answer, which you know by now, was the bottom one. Surprising right? I just said that comment about your brother, and now I am saying anyone outside of your house can drive with your permission? This rule of insurance is a tricky one and is not even cut in stone depending on the situation.

Many times, when filing the claim after an accident, an insurance adjuster will ask the driver if he lives with the policy holder. In this circumstance, the common sense answer is "Yes, I do" because logically the driver thinks, "I am supposed to be living with the policy holder to be allowed to drive." But that is where the driver seals your fate. The driver said he lives with you, but he is not listed on your policy; that means he is not covered.

I am not telling you this so that you can lie and get out of a sticky situation. I wouldn't do that. I am telling you because this rule of insurance actually works to your advantage in most cases. If your sister is in town for a couple days, but you are going to be working, she can borrow your car for a bit. Maybe, your car broke down and your neighbor said you can borrow his car, no problem as long as the use isn't every day for months on end.

This sounds pretty straight forward though right? It's not. With insurance, the situation is almost never so straight forward. Let's say you're engaged and your fiancé does not live with you, but he borrows your car every day while you're at work to pick up your kid from school. I would love to say you're covered, but you're not.

The insurance adjuster might say, "He was driving your car every day, so he should have been listed as a driver. We will not cover this accident." Trailing into this grey area is the constant fear we have as insurance agents because, technically, you are not breaking the rules by not listing your fiancé who does not live with you. On the other hand, you are breaking the rules because your fiancé drives your car daily.

In the end, I go with the side of caution and suggest to add him to your policy. This has negative connotations though because it can look like I am just trying to get more money out of you, when really I am afraid of your life getting ruined over a grey area with no defined line. And I know that if I call the insurance company, no matter what the situation, they will want me to add that person who is potentially going to be driving your car even once a week, but the company says that because they want the money.

What do I do if I get in an accident?

Below is a step-by-step process that I created for my own customers:

1. <u>Call the police, no matter what</u>. This practice is to protect you legally. The other person could be nice at the scene and then call your insurance company a couple days later to complain about you. The law will sort out fault and liability. *Keep communication with the other driver to a minimum so what you say does not get used against you*

2. <u>Do not admit fault and do not blame the other driver either</u> when the police arrive on the scene. Only state the facts.

3. <u>Pick up your police report</u>. The police at the scene will give you a report number and tell you how to get one. It usually takes three to five days for the report to be ready. Read the police report to find out who is deemed responsible for the accident.

4. <u>Contact your insurance agent</u>. Let him know you need a "Certificate of Compliance" sent to the BMV or DMV (depending where you live) to notify the state that you were covered that day. This will avoid any complications with your license.

5. <u>Do what your agent suggests</u>. Protecting you is our job. We are paid to help you work through these confusing situations. I don't mean we do all the work for you, what I mean is that we give you informed advice about the next steps to take. An agent will usually tell you to do 1 of 3 things. If the police report says you were at fault, you can wait to see if the other driver files a claim against your insurance company. If the other driver was at fault, you need to call his insurance com-

pany to file a claim. If the other driver was at fault but did not have insurance, you'll have to decide if you want to file an uninsured motorist claim with your own insurance company. If the damages were small, you may not want to file a claim because once you call to file a claim, your renewal price will go up because you now have an accident on your record. If the accident was bad, you should get your car fixed, and your insurance company will sue the driver who wronged you.

Note: Most claims adjusters will not call you back within 24 hours of leaving a message. Some of them will take more than 48 hours to return your call. You will need to practice a bit of patience in the midst of a claim.

Does "Non-owners" mean I can drive anyone's vehicle?

Yes, this coverage means you can drive anyone's vehicle with exception to any vehicles you own yourself. The problem though is that your coverage is your coverage, and if you are driving a borrowed 2015 Ford Fusion, the vehicle will only be covered for Liability.

Non-owner's policies only cover Liability and sometimes Uninsured Motorist, but the coverage depends on the insurance company you have the policy with.

Another circumstance where this coverage will not work for you is when you are driving a vehicle that is uninsured. You will be fine legally, but the owner of the vehicle will likely lose his license for not having insurance on his vehicle. This is another of those grey areas I've mentioned before.

Non-owner's policies are not designed for the every-day driver. These policies' main purpose is for a person who lost his license and wants to get it back with an SR-22 but does not own a vehicle. Typically, you'd want to get this policy if your job requires you have a valid license even though you don't own a vehicle.

Why is insurance so expensive?

I love tough questions like this. We all have a different perspective on what is considered "expensive." I consider $200 expensive, but some customers have to pay $300-$400, so "expensive" is a relative term that is directly related to your circumstances.

I will say, rates change constantly, and that change is due in a large portion to crime. By crime, I mean not only hit & runs and stolen cars but also uninsured drivers. A big part of the rate changes are due to uninsured motorist in your zip code.

If more people are driving without insurance, the insurance company pays more money out to uninsured motorist claims, and the company will most likely never get that money back from suing the other driver.

Are insurance companies making as much money as everyone says?

No. According to WellPoint Inc., a large insurance company which owns the well-known Blue Cross and Blue Shield Indiana and California departments, they only profit about 5% each year. This is tiny, especially compared to Apple, who has an 18% profit margin in 2016 by June. The insurance companies released their finances to the S.E.C. showing detailed growth and loss ratios. It was determined that the larger portion of that profit was made on wise investments that pay them back.

Some insurance companies have higher profits, some lower, but the average profit comes out to 5%. This profit margin is common for most insurance companies, and since a tornado could wipe out 5,000 houses in a single afternoon, causing an insurance company to suddenly have to pay out tens of millions, the profit margin is scarily close to the red.

Do I need to list permit drivers on my policy before letting them drive my car?

Usually yes, but some insurance companies do not require them to be listed. On the other side, some insurance companies do not allow permit drivers at all. I wish I could give black or white answers, but you're probably noticing there are exceptions to everything in insurance. Ask your insurance agent before allowing them to drive the vehicle and always be in the vehicle with them when they are driving.

How can I reach you if I have questions?

I have Twitter, a YouTube channel, and if your question really important or private, you can reach someone who has the proverbial bat signal for me by emailing angelinshobart@gmail.com.

Here are some of the links to reach me at:

www.Angelinshobart.com

www.facebook.com/angelautohobart

Search "angel auto insurance" on YouTube (we are the only channel by that name)

My twitter handle is @martinglennon

Does Angel Auto Insurance only sell Auto Insurance?

We have had that name for 20 years, and the name is well known in my area now. The name has stuck with the people around my agency, but we have been offering just about any kind of insurance for the last 10 years. My specialty is Business Insurance. I have agents who specialized in Health & Life insurance and Home & Auto insurance, as well as recreational vehicles when requested.

Your Next Steps

I wish I could stand up right now and clap for you. In fact, I will ... there you go!

This may sound tacky, but I'm very proud of you! Did you know that 9 out of 10 book buyers never read past the first chapter? It's amazing, but it's true. You're different, and I applaud you for that.

You're no longer blind about insurance and what companies and agents are doing to unsuspecting consumers. You now know what questions to ask your insurance company and your agent to know if you're getting the best deal. You now know if they're playing games with you and 'scamming' you. And ultimately, you now know whether you should trust them or not.

In addition, you now know the answers to commonly asked insurance questions and how to immediately save money on your insurance policy.

Now, here's what I suggest you do next. First, read back through this book and make notes of where you can save immediately. Call your agent now (or change agents if you can't trust yours) to save money where you can, so you can start saving for your future.

Second, do not keep this information to yourself. Spread the word, and get this information into your family members' and friends' hands. They need to know what you know, and they need to know that they can save too.

Take action now, and let me know how much you're saving. I'd love to hear from you! You can reach me via email at angelinshobart@gmail.com.

~Martin J. Glennon

P.S. There's no doubt that there will be many agents and companies who do not like what I'm saying. But their opinions don't matter. I didn't write this book for them. I wrote this book for you and your loved ones, so take action and pass this book onto someone you love.

P.P.S. If you're interested in learning more about how to save, how to protect your family, and how you can help me change the way insurance is done, you can find me here:

www.Angelinshobart.com

www.facebook.com/angelautohobart

Search "angel auto insurance" on YouTube (we are the only channel by that name)

My twitter handle is @martinglennon

About the Author

Martin Glennon owns Angel Auto Insurance in Hobart, Indiana. He started working in an insurance agency when he was just a boy. He took ownership of the insurance agency in 2015, like his father and grandfather before him.

Insurance runs in his family, and Martin has made the business successful enough to fund the non-profit work he always dreamed about undertaking, such as feeding the needy and teaching young locals how to live successful and fulfilling lives full of integrity.

While the name Angel Auto Insurance implies the company does only auto insurance, Martin specializes in Business Insurance and has agents who specialize in Health & Life insurance as well as Home & Auto Insurance.

Martin started working in his dad's office at the age of eight, filing and working to save up for different things. Martin and his team have written over 10,000 insurance policies since he took over in 2014, and he is uniquely qualified to offer insider information about the insurance industry and where the industry is headed.

Martin has lofty goals, is an aspiring business speaker, and often mentors business owners seeking better direction for their companies.

Martin J. Glennon

During his time off, Martin spends time with family, focuses on reading and self-improvement, and attends conferences about time management, real estate, and insurance.

You can reach Martin on:

www.Angelinshobart.com

www.facebook.com/angelautohobart

Search "angel auto insurance" on YouTube

@martinglennon on Twitter

www.ingramcontent.com/pod-product-compliance
Lightning Source LLC
Chambersburg PA
CBHW070253230526
45470CB00002B/584